dismantling

the

fantasy

an invitation to the fullness of life

Darryl Bailey

NON-DUALITY PRESS

Editor: Sandra Stuart

Layout: Link Phillips, Julian Noyce & John Gustard

ISBN: 978-0-9563091-6-7

introduction

There are no traditions in this.
It is not an attempt to convince or to convert.
It is a dream questioning itself.

the cloud

Once upon a time, a group of friends lay on a hillside
watching a cloud. They had become fascinated with
its appearance while walking in the country. It was a
marvellous cloud, massive and surging, one moment
appearing to be a house and the next a bevy of balloons.
In turn there were forests and cities, animals and people,
comings and goings, no end of activity.

As it so happened, an old man, a stranger, was wandering
close by. When the group of friends saw him, they cried
out in their excitement, *Old man, come join us! Come
watch this cloud!*

After hurried introductions and the shifting of bodies, he
took his place within the group.

The afternoon passed pleasantly as the cloud continued
to surprise. There were soldiers at war and children at

play. There were creatures of the wild: birds, mammals, and fish, as well as beasts of work and burden. There was a mother and her child. There were the many scenes of life: birth, death, sickness, youth and old age. There were lovers and fighters, friends and enemies, the interaction of groups, and single, poignant portraits.

Time wore on, the afternoon dwindled, and eventually the old man stood to leave. He thanked his new friends and made his goodbyes, but hesitated, looking at the gathering.

May I ask you a question?

Of course, they replied, in their various ways.

Were you at all concerned for those we saw this afternoon?

Who? they asked.

The figures we saw in the cloud: the soldiers, the animals, the children.

The friends looked at each other, perplexed.

One answered, *Old man, there were no people, no animals; there was only the cloud.*

The others nodded in agreement.

> *How do you know that?*

How do we know what?

> *How do you know there was only the cloud?*

It's obvious, anyone can see it.

> *See what?*

There is only the cloud; it's still there.

> *What about the forms we saw?*

There were no forms; there is only the cloud and it has no particular form.

> *How do you know that?*

Just look, and you can see it.

What do you see?

There are no forms there.

How do you know that?

Because they're always changing. No form is ever really there; whatever form you think you see is always altering, rearranging in some way.

How do you know that?

Just look! That's all you have to do.

There were no soldiers, no animals, no children?

No. It may have seemed like that, but there was only the cloud.

There were no soldiers deciding to fight, no lovers deciding to love?

How could those false appearances decide to do anything? There is only the movement of the cloud.

So the cloud decides to move?

No. The cloud does not decide to move. It has no form. It simply moves. That's its nature.

How do you know that?

Have you ever seen a cloud that stopped changing? Every aspect of it is shifting in some way. It doesn't decide to do it; it's on automatic. The movement simply happens.

There were no people?
There was no birth and death?

Birth and death of what? There is only the cloud. It seems like many forms coming and going, but it's always only the unformed cloud.

And no one is deciding to do anything?

No. The forms that appear to be there are not really there, because each one is altering in some way and eventually disappears. There is simply action or motion. The forms are not the reality; they are false appearances. There is only movement, a streaming that has no particular form.

But the lovers who moved closer together …?

There were no lovers, no soldiers, no animals. There is only the cloud.

The old man pondered this slowly.

> There were no forms there?
> No decisions to act?
> No birth and death?

That's right! said the friends, thinking they had finally gotten through to him.

> But how do you know that for certain?

Just watch! The forms that you see are changing all the time. They never stop. No particular form is ever really there. If you had to describe a cloud, you wouldn't say it looked like a horse or a soldier. That wouldn't give you a true sense of the cloud. A cloud is constantly changing.

The appearance of form is not the reality. The altering is. That's the basic fact. There is no coming or going, no birth or death, no decisions being made, no matter how much it seems like that. There is only motion. Anyone can see that if they watch it long enough.

The old man considered this carefully.

You're absolutely certain?

Yes! We're absolutely certain.

And you can tell all of this from seeing this constant change, this motion, this dynamic?

Yes.

The old man contemplated this.

May I ask another question?

The friends remained silent, waiting.

Are you actually people?

What are you talking about? Of course we're people.

But you're changing.

What?

Everything you are – your bodies, thoughts, emotions,

interests, urges, desires, capacities, decisions, focuses, ideas, activities – in fact, more than just you, all things that you know of.

What about them?

They're constantly changing.

Yes, sighed the members of the group, *They're changing.*

Do you change them?

No, old man, they simply ...

The friends stood staring at him, their minds racing, exploding to find some other response.

He gazed back at them.

They looked.

He looked.

For what seemed to be a very, very, long time.

Then he smiled, turned, and wandered away.

dialogue one

Q: *Good morning.*

DB: Good morning.

Q: *I want to ask you some questions regarding your perspective on life. I've heard some of it already, but there are certain aspects I want to clarify.*

DB: Okay, but this is simply my perspective. I don't ask anyone to believe it and I don't expect anyone else to approach life in this way.

Q: *I understand that. Perhaps I can begin by asking if you see yourself as a spiritual teacher.*

DB: No.

Q: *But you give spiritual teachings at a local yoga centre.*

DB: Not exactly. A number of years ago, I was invited to offer my perspective in that setting. It's an examination of our direct experience of the moment, in order to discover if the ideas we have about life are actually matching our experience.

Q: *Though much of what you say sounds like the teachings of Buddhism, Taoism, Advaita, and some others.*

DB: Yes, in some instances even Christianity. There are portions of those traditions that sound very similar to what I'm saying as well as portions that don't.

Q: *But you spent years exploring those traditions. You were a monk; you lived with well-known Buddhist teachers; and you spent time with independent teachers who were generally considered to be enlightened.*

DB: Yes. From a very early age, there seemed to be something odd in the process of perception, something I couldn't quite clarify, and this is what attracted me to various meditation traditions and teachers, because they expressed an interest in examining the process of perception. Over the years there were many of them.

This current situation at the yoga centre offers the

chance for others to investigate their experience. And there are lots of surprises for anyone who wants to join in.

It began as an exploration with one friend and has now grown to a larger situation. There are a number of people who say they find it supportive in their daily lives.

Some tell me it's a very clear consideration of life. Some say it explains all the traditional spiritual teachings. And some say it's really off the mark.

I'm not concerned with any of that. I'm interested in a certain kind of freedom that sometimes arises in this exploration.

Q: Can you describe that freedom?

DB: No. The most profound aspects of freedom turn away from defining life. There is eventually no belief in the stories of thought. They're needed for functioning, but the obsessive urge to explain existence falls away.

There's no way to convey this freedom by focusing on more explanations.

Q: Some say if we drop the focus on perception and thought, we come to pure awareness, or pure consciousness. Do you agree?

DB: No. That's just another thought. These are incorrect assumptions about existence. No one ever left the womb thinking they were an awareness or a consciousness. It takes a long time for society to program us to think like that.

People often object to this kind of statement, saying that to dismiss such things is nihilistic, useless, life denying, and even damaging.

Q: Isn't it?

DB: Not in my experience. A reaction like that indicates they don't understand what I'm pointing to.

People desperately want to describe existence and, historically, they speak of matter, energy, consciousness, spirit, oneness, and mystery. But descriptions are merely limited interpretations. All of them. They can never tell us what life actually is.

I say there is no matter, energy, consciousness, spirit,

oneness, or mystery. This is often misunderstood, because people think it's saying there's nothing at all, and that sounds very bleak.

To say that life is not mystery, not oneness, not consciousness, not any thing, this is not the same as saying there's nothing. It's not pointing to some state of oblivion or bleak emptiness. In fact it's just the opposite.

Try asking a newborn baby whether there is awareness or consciousness. Ask an infant if a world exists. Awareness, consciousness, and world are merely labels taught to us by society long after we leave the womb. For a newborn, there are no things, no definable forms, no labels, no awareness, no body, no mind, and no world.

However, this doesn't mean there's nothing. I don't have the impression that a newborn baby is feeling lost and bleak without ideas of awareness, consciousness, or the many other things of life.

An infant is a vital, pulsing event – lively, sensitive, alert, and highly responsive. There's nothing nihilistic in that.

Ideas don't tell us what life is. They don't even focus on life. They focus on abstract notions of division and comparison, dividing life's constantly vibrant movement into false impressions of static form, describing one false form as different from another.

That's how we get the impression of understanding something; it's one form, or thing, as opposed to some other form, or thing.

But calling one portion of the moment "awareness", and another portion "the object of awareness", never tells us what the basic happening is. Instead, it gives the mistaken impression that this happening is divided into different forms that can be understood.

When you're one hour old, you're not thinking you're an awareness experiencing a world. According to research into child development, it takes seven years to be fully trained to think like that.

You may think I'm ultimately saying life is a mystery, but I'm not. "Life" and "mystery" are just more labels. To me this is not about coming up with another label. It's not about fixating on another thought. It's about dropping the obsession with thought, by seeing its limitations.

Q: *If we drop the focus on thought, what are we left with?*

DB: Motion, expressing itself.

Q: *Motion.*

DB: Yes. Life is motion accomplishing itself.
Perception and thought give us descriptions of form,
but at the same time they tell us that forms can't be
real. If you observe any form, you find that it's always
changing, so it isn't a particular form at all. It's a process,
a movement, an action.

The world of perception and thought turns against its
own stories and states they can't be true. Everyone's
experience of life indicates that motion is truer than the
perception of form.

A thorough investigation reveals that all things are
changing, and eventually replaces the impression of form
with a sense of motion that has no particular shape.

This action or motion isn't dependent on having a name.
At birth we have no labels and life functions anyway.
Our so-called bodies and actions function automatically,
in an amazingly vital way.

Our heads bob; our arms and legs move; we cry; we feed

at our mother's breast; and eventually we crawl. We don't plan these things. We don't think them out. There is a mysterious, spontaneous functioning, moving on its own. That's all there is at delivery and that's all there is now.

Descriptions of life make no sense at all. Ideas of different forms in existence, such as objects, events, and beings, are the same as ideas of forms in clouds. Clouds don't have a form.

If people tried to convince you that the shapes in a cloud are a stable world, with beings and things, you would say it isn't true, because those shapes are obviously fleeting. There is no form there. It only appears to be there. I'm pointing out that it's the same with all of existence.

A mountain is certainly thicker than a cloud, but, like the cloud, it has no lasting shape. I'm not concerned with whether rock seems more substantial than mist. What's important to me is that neither one has form. Each is always changing and will eventually appear to disappear.

Existence has no shape, so it can't be understood as anything in particular.

This seems important to note because most people are caught in ideas of cultivating some understanding of existence, in order to bring an end to conflict. Even though perception may be useful to a limited degree, it's ultimately a focus on forms where no forms actually exist; therefore, it's a focus on delusion.

It's the frustrating attempt to impose form on motion, the attempt to hold life still, mentally and physically, when life will always push beyond those imposed boundaries. This attempt to resist life's movement is conflict; it can't bring an end to conflict.

The obsessive focus on ideas of form is always frustrating, and it makes it impossible to realize something else.

Q: Which is?

DB: That everything is indefinable motion. There's no indication anywhere that we govern this action, because we obviously don't create our own movement. We don't create the ongoing, ever-changing movement of our needs, interests, urges, abilities, inclinations, and potential.

The fantasy forms in a cloud do not direct the action

of that cloud and the fantasy forms in existence do not direct the action of existence.

Q: But this is another thought.

DB: Yes. That's why I say I can't describe the most profound aspects of freedom. The most that perception and thought can do is reveal their own contradictions. Thought simply realizes that it can't describe what we actually experience. Even the idea of experience doesn't apply.

If that realization arises, the obsessive focus on perception and thought is dropped. The action that we call perception and thought continues to present itself, but it's a happening that can't be explained in any way at all.

Q: How do we get to that?

DB: We don't have to get to it; we never left it. We are that. All we have to do is wake up to it. Actually, no one needs to wake up to it, but life may unfold in that direction, whether you like it or not.

When you ask, "How do we get to that?", you're assuming

that we're an awareness in a body that can influence life, and that somehow we've lost something we need to get back to, that somehow we're separated from our wholeness, separated from our true potential. But all of that is an illusion based on the appearance of forms.

Existence is motion. Whatever we are now, whatever we're doing now, is an inexplicable movement accomplishing itself. Nothing can be added to it and nothing can be taken away from it.

When I speak of this mysterious action or movement, I'm not pointing to something that we need to develop or cultivate, nor am I pointing to something we need to get to. I'm simply saying this is what already is.

The people who are trying to get rich or become famous are simply moved that way. And the people who lead charitable lives or undergo an apparent spiritual awakening are moved in that way.

Q: But it's influenced by various things, by people and events.

DB: It appears that way, but if we examine the behaviour of those various things, people, and events, we find they're compelled to move in the way they do, by their intrinsic nature. And we're compelled to respond to them in the way we do, by our intrinsic nature.

It's changing all the time. Usually in subtle ways, but sometimes radically. We're not locked into one mode of responding. The manner in which this happening will display itself next is ultimately unpredictable. There are general patterns, but they never repeat themselves exactly.

As a newborn, there was a mysterious happening that required no wilful effort or understanding. This has never left. There was no you doing anything then. There is no you doing anything now.

Q: How would someone live with that sense of things?

DB: Just as we are now. There isn't anyone doing the seeing, hearing, touching, tasting, smelling and thinking. It's an automatic functioning. There actually isn't any seeing, hearing, touching, tasting, smelling or thinking. These are acquired labels and mistaken notions of division and form.

What we call our biology – our neurology, our glands,

our brains, our hearts – these are functioning automatically. They're a process accomplishing itself. Your heart isn't asking, "How should I beat?" It's simply moving.

You might tell me that you're different from your heart, that you are "self-aware" or "self-conscious" and your heart isn't. I'm saying that no one is self-aware or self-conscious. The idea of a self that is knowing existence, or directing the movement of existence, is a delusion of thought. It's "self-delusion".

If you sit down and make no effort at all, life happens anyway. The ever-shifting process that you are simply functions. The heart keeps beating, the breath keeps breathing, the moods keep mooding. Thoughts and urges come and go. Some are followed. Some are not. This dynamic simply happens.

At some point you will stand up, you will go the toilet, you will eat, sleep, work, relate to others; you will relate to the world in the only way that feels right to you or makes sense to you.

When I say "feels right" or "makes sense", I don't just mean intellectually, but also emotionally, physically, spiritually, and psychologically – the entire package. You will act in the only way you can. There is no you that can stop it or guide it. Everything you are is simply this mysterious happening.

We have always been an inexplicable dynamic. There is no person and no thing separate from this dynamic.

Q: *What about free will?*

DB: The descriptions of a self and a world, of doing and being, of past, present, and future, path and goal, ignorance and enlightenment, free will and fate – these ideas do not apply to what is. They're built around ideas of form, and we can't find any stable form.

Q: *But we can't live without thought.*

DB: No, and we don't have to, but perhaps we can stop believing its delusions.

A map may be useful at times, but you don't believe that a map is actually the land that it describes. When you go on vacation, you don't spread a map on the floor, sit on it, and think you've gone somewhere.

Thoughts may also be useful, but focusing on the stories of thought, and believing they're explaining a reality, is exactly the same as sitting on a map and thinking you've gone somewhere.

Q: *So, this unformed happening – what is it?*

DB: There's no way of saying.

Q: *Well then, what's it doing?*

DB: There's no way of saying.

Q: *I find that hard to accept.*

DB: This isn't about acceptance. It's about acknowledging life as it is.

All that's ever known are descriptions of form where no form actually exists. These descriptions may be helpful at times, but they're ultimately meaningless. There can be no true description of anything.

When we came out of the womb, there was this –
    [D gestures to everything around.]
It had no name and no particular sense of form. Now

23

there's the mistaken impression that it has name and form, and we think that's reality.

Freedom has nothing to do with developing acceptance. We like to have cozy stories. One of them is that we're someone on a journey to some wonderful spiritual goal and we slowly develop our spiritual capacity to attain that goal. But the idea that there is a path, a goal, and someone walking the path, is false.

Life isn't definable.

People often think they can let their senses experience the world purely, that they can come to some kind of pure knowing, without thought. But the idea of the senses and something being sensed, the idea of pure knowing, is just another thought.

There is the desire to be a "knowing" and to have something to "know", to have an "observer" and something "observed". But these ideas of form and separation are false. There's just this –

[D gestures to everything around and to himself.]
It's empty of form. It's empty of message.

Q: *But how do you know that?*

DB: The world of thought may eventually realize that its descriptions don't apply. The statement that they don't apply is simply perception and thought pointing to their many contradictions.

The illusion realizes its stories can't be true, and the obsessive focus on those fantasies falls away.

Q: *How do I see the indefinable motion?*

DB: If we sit down and give up all efforts to do anything – if we make no effort to think or to act – motion will reveal itself. The movement that we are, and the larger movement that existence is, will simply present itself. It's quite obvious.

Body sensations, thoughts, emotions, interests, urges, mental activities and so on, present themselves automatically, without conscious effort, without a director. Even the sense of conscious effort and direction arises without effort.

Everything we observe is changing in some way. If all forms are changing, it becomes obvious that existence has no particular form.

Q: Why do we think we're separate from it and somehow doing it?

DB: There's no explanation for that. Most people are simply not interested in examining these false views. Some people find it incredibly important and others do not.

Q: What about concentration?

DB: Concentration?

Q: Yes, the cultivation of concentration. How important is that?

DB: If it's important to you, I would say it's important. If not, then it isn't important.

Q: But as far as spiritual awakening is concerned.

DB: There isn't any awakening.

Q: No awakening?

DB: Descriptions don't apply to what's happening here, not even the description of spiritual awakening.

Q: But to know that is awakening.

DB: No. To know that descriptions don't apply is the end of belief in any description.

The words "descriptions do not apply" are not describing anything. Thought is simply realizing its limitations.

The dream is dismantling itself, but that does not say anything about what actually is. The attempt to describe any existence stops, because the belief that it can be described ends. Even the description of awakening is dismissed.

We are always personalizing, historacizing, psychologizing, scientizing, philosophizing, spiritualizing, and so on. All of these are false stories.

Q: So even this discussion is ridiculous.

DB: I wouldn't say it's ridiculous. It simply happens. There's no way of knowing what's going on here. We can call it a conversation between two people, but that's false, and there's no way of giving any true description.

Q: Well, then, what about the development of

concentration as a method for awakening?

DB: The idea that you need to practice something for a
so-called awakening to occur is based on the fantasy that
there is a you controlling a world.

But the belief in that fantasy has to end for any so-called
awakening to occur, because stories about forms of any
kind are false.

You don't need to be highly concentrated to discover that
descriptions don't apply. You just need to be interested in
exploring this.

There is the general impression that life is divided into
separate forms and that you are a form that needs to
manipulate other forms in order to experience union,
completion, or wholeness. But all of that is fantasy.

We may start out thinking that we need to develop
ourselves in order to get something called awakening
or enlightenment. But, if it's seen that the stories of
form are false, then there is no longer any ignorance or
awakening, path or goal, journey or arrival – no you, no
me, no world, no birth, no death. All of that only exists
in fantasy, the world of description.

Q: But this observation is also a description.

DB: Yes, it's the world of perception and thought pointing to its own delusion. If it becomes very clear, you can then drop the obsessive focus on that delusion.

This moment is a mysterious, vital, radiant expression. No one is doing this expression. It's accomplishing itself. Seeing is expressing itself. Hearing is expressing itself. Tactile sensations are expressing themselves. Thought simply arises. The heart beats, hair grows, food digests. The sun rises, the planets turn, the seasons come and go. All of this occurs automatically.

This motion is the basis of what we all experience. No one is doing it. It can't be stopped. It has no particular form.

No effort is needed for this dynamic to occur. No one has to work to get to this. Everything is already this. There isn't anything that can be separated from this. Nothing can lose this; nothing can gain this. There is only this –

[D gestures to everything around and to himself.]
And this has no form.

Out of this mysterious, unformed happening apparently rises the notion of form, and the stories begin. The focus isn't on the unformed actuality, the constant motion. Instead, the focus is on illusions of shape.

The illusions say, "I am an individual form, separate from all the other forms in life, and I have lost something important. I have lost my wholeness, my truth, my completeness, my perfection, and I must search to find happiness. I need to manipulate the world, develop my self, purify myself, and pursue some obscure future goal of union, completion, or enlightenment, in order to regain whatever it is I feel I am missing or I have lost."

But all of this is a fantasy. In the same way that the apparent forms of a cloud are not the true, unformed nature of the cloud, the apparent forms of existence are not its true nature.

There is no stable form that could be classified as a separate self doing its life. There is no form that has lost anything, that has gone the wrong way, or been separated from wholeness or truth.

In the stories built around the false appearance of form, there is the journey of a self through a physical world over time. There seem to be encounters with family and friends, parents, teachers, employers, spiritual guides, and so on.

There is a focus on these false descriptions of a self doing things in a so-called world. There is a sense of separation, alienation, and dissatisfaction, along with the urge to create union and fulfilment.

But there is an unavoidable frustration in this, because the fantasy of a self can never overcome the feelings of separation, alienation, and dissatisfaction. The fantasy of a self builds those feelings.

Instead of acknowledging a great, indefinable happening, we fantasize separation, a self desperately searching for union or completion.

So the fantasy self pursues its desire for wholeness. It pursues relationship, money, power, education, psychology, therapy, religion, spirituality, yoga techniques, meditation techniques, insight, understanding, and so on.

But the sense of completion never comes with any of this, because the fantasy of a self cultivating wholeness can't get rid of the sense of fragmentation and lack.

That fantasy is the sense of fragmentation and lack.

Perhaps, at some point, we begin to question the ideas of form and personal doing. The story of a self doing its life will not stand up to serious examination, and the fantasy will dismantle itself.

Life is then without any message. This is not a romantic state of knowing a great mystery. Instead, thought is thoroughly stumped. There is complete and utter puzzlement.

The effort to know, and to do, stops and, surprisingly, existence carries on. Everything proceeds without any imposed effort or understanding.

What is called perception, thought, and wilful effort still occurs, but it's obviously an indefinable movement accomplishing itself.

This mysterious happening carries no sense of fragmentation or lack.

Right now, if you make no effort at all, there is what we call the happening of this moment – what we call the body, mind, awareness, thoughts, feelings, emotions, interests, urges, aptitudes and abilities, as well as everything else. This happening simply happens.

It's not necessary to dwell on defining this happening. The entire process orchestrates itself.

In acknowledging this, there is no personal anguish, no focus on fantasized ideas of a "you" who is suffering, searching, doing, failing, and losing; no need to move to fullness, truth, union, completion, and satisfaction. There are no self-aggrandizing stories of accomplishment and superiority.

There is simply a mysterious process accomplishing itself.

Q: Is it some unfeeling state?

DB: No. Everything you usually interpret as "you" – the body, mind, thoughts, feelings, interests, loves, concerns, urges, efforts, and actions – those still happen, but there's no longer any belief in those descriptions. There's no need to think there is a you doing anything or missing anything.

There is simply a mysterious, radiant, pulsing event. A miraculous presentation. An endlessly exotic parade.

Throughout life we're always thinking in terms of ownership. We're always thinking, "This is my life, my body, my wife, my husband, my thoughts, my emotions, my doing, my spiritual journey, my insights," and so on.

"I" have a certain amount of time here and "I" must use "my" will to choose to do something useful with "my" life. And that leads to "my" successes and "my" failures.

But no owner exists. If we examine the happening that life is, the happening is obvious, but there isn't any owner, or any stable thing to be owned.

Q: You're asking me to stop believing any idea I've ever had.

DB: No. I'm not asking you to do anything. I'm simply offering my perspective.

However, if you're interested in examining your ideas of reality, they will eventually have to be rejected, along with every idea that humankind has ever had. Because they describe forms that no one can actually find. Forms are motion.

There are those who say that since all views are merely

relative viewpoints, they're all relatively true, but this is not so. Since all views are based on forms that no one can find, none of them apply.

What is is a happening that refuses description of any kind. A dynamic that requires no conscious effort or understanding.

When this perspective is offered, it sounds as though it's describing existence, but it's not. It's dismantling all descriptions.

The real isn't found in forms and labels. Describing a form that doesn't exist, and giving it a name, doesn't tell us anything about anything.

Even though descriptions may be useful at times, they are a totally distorted impression of what's happening here.

Q: All of this sounds right to me, but I'm getting confused. At the same time that it makes sense to say there is no possible understanding, I can feel myself wanting to understand, in order to get free. It's as though the mind wants to sneak up on itself even when it knows it doesn't exist.

DB: Yes, that's the power of delusion. It can see its own fantasy and yet wants to go on attaching to it. This is natural, so I would suggest that you not fight it. There's no need to force this. It's enough to get a basic sense of it. If it makes sense to you, the dismantling will happen on its own.

To begin, it requires nothing more than listening to this view I'm offering. This view is also a fantasy, but it will dismantle itself.

We can stop for now and, if you're still interested, we can pick it up again tomorrow.

For now you can set it aside;
relax,
go for a walk,
have something to eat,
whatever seems appropriate.

dialogue two

DB: Good morning.

Q: *Good morning.*

DB: How are you?

Q: *I'm fine, but I'm still confused.*

DB: That's natural. The important aspect of this investigation is to keep it simple. We're usually so absorbed in complicated stories that it's difficult to come back to basics.

There is a wrong assumption about life that occurs at the most basic level of perception. That wrong assumption contains a huge amount of mental anguish.

No matter how much I say this, it has no value unless you

can see it in your own experience. So let's look at that.

Everyone's experience of existence is the happening
of the present moment. It doesn't matter who you are,
the present moment is your basic sense of life. Even if
you're remembering the past or imagining the future, it's
happening now.

Everyone has a sense of being – the impression that
something is present now, existing now, happening now.

This sense of existing disappears on a regular basis.
Whether we like it or not, the sense of existing
disappears every day. We call that sleep.

Sleep automatically moves into dreaming, and dreaming
moves on to become deep sleep. Deep sleep eventually
moves into waking up, and there is a vague sense of
having had a good or bad night. All of this happens
without your efforts. In fact, you can't stop it from
happening.

Your most basic sense of life presents itself as a constant
movement: waking, dreaming, sleeping; waking,
dreaming, sleeping; and so on. Each state moves through
its various stages to complete its cycle.

In the sleep state, there is no sense of form, not even a sense of "being". In the dream state, the apparent forms are obviously fleeting. They are not what we would call reality. In the waking state, however, it appears that there are real forms.

But, if we bother to pay attention to them, every form that we see, hear, touch, taste, smell, and mentally observe, is also changing. Sights, sounds, touches, tastes, smells, and mental activities, are constantly altering. Some slowly; some quickly.

More than that, the senses themselves are shifting. Seeing, hearing, touching, tasting, smelling, and thinking are constantly shifting predominance. Awareness doesn't have a particular form. One moment there is seeing; the next, hearing; the next, thinking; and so on.

At times, there is a sense of clear attention, and at other times the attention wanders; it's foggy and dull. Attention may be broad and expansive or narrow and tightly focused. It might be open and receiving or refusing and resistant. It's constantly shifting.

Added to this, the sense organs are altering. It doesn't matter who you are, every portion of your body is altering as it either matures or degenerates. Not only can we view this in our bathroom mirror, but scientists tell us that, over the course of seven years, every cell in the body is replaced. Every cell dies and is replaced.

It doesn't matter if you're a Christian, a Buddhist, a Hindu, a Jew, a Muslim, or a scientist, an artist, a businessperson, a philosopher, and so on, this fact of change is ultimately your experience.

The sense organs, the senses, and all the objects ever sensed, have no particular form. Even if you've never paid any attention to this, with a serious investigation it becomes obvious.

It doesn't matter whether we're talking about thoughts, emotions, bodies, the weather, a house, a mountain, a planet, or a galaxy – every thing is changing – even as we consider it.

It becomes obvious that existence is not just changing; it's constantly changing. Things that change very slowly, such as a house, a mountain, or a solar system, do not stay exactly the same for hundreds of years and then grow old overnight. They are shifting now, and, even though we can't see every subtle movement, there is the impression that they are changing in small ways.

They're flowing. Very slowly.

In faster movements, such as the flow of consciousness, there appear to be many individual thoughts arising and passing, but try to stop one of those thoughts, to simply observe it, and we find no solid object, only a continuous streaming, like smoke. That streaming will even disappear as we attempt to watch it.

Even though we have the impression that individual thoughts are there, there is only a constant altering.

In swirling smoke, it's quite obvious that, even as we attempt to identify a particular pattern or form in the movement, the pattern has already changed. Obviously, no particular object exists in that motion; there is only a continuously streaming display.

Mountains are more deceptive, but they're also changing. Just because a mountain flows at a much slower rate does not mean that it has any more form than smoke. Mountains become hills, and eventually fade away. The amazing thing about this is that everyone experiences this fact of change, this streaming, without seeing its significance.

We are forever complaining about our behaviour, our health, our relationships, our work, the economy, the educational system, the government, and so on, and the complaints centre on the fact that all things, for periods of time, change in ways that are unpleasant.

We cling to the illusion of form, physical forms, mental forms, emotional forms, situational forms, structural forms, temporal forms, and relational forms, but they never stop changing. So we complain.

No matter how much we want to cling to an apparent form of health, mood, state of mind, behaviour, relationship, understanding, career, and so on, it alters. Because existence has no particular form.

Here we find the basic agony of life. We believe there are stable forms when, in fact, there is merely unstoppable, unpredictable motion.

If forms are described, whether mental, physical, emotional, structural, situational, temporal, relational, and so on, they are essentially an illusion.

We attempt to impose form where no form exists.

Since portions of existence move at different rates, some fast and some slow, certain aspects appear to be relatively solid and stable, and it is beneficial, in a limited way, to identify them as separate forms and to speak as if those forms actually exist.

Identifying forms in smoke isn't that important, but it's very helpful to identify the form of a salt shaker, a person, a car, or a mountain, even though they, like swirls in smoke, will eventually fade away.

It's also beneficial to identify various cycles in movement. One such cycle is a rhythm of highs and lows. To note this general rhythm is helpful, because we don't get overly concerned when life is on a downward trend. All we need to do is wait. An upward trend is coming at some point.

Q: But any form we try to describe would actually be false, because it's constantly altering. And anything we cling to eventually brings conflict because it's changing beyond our control.

DB: Yes. And more importantly, no one is doing this

43

movement. We could say it happens automatically, because it simply happens.

No one is doing it, and no one can stop it.

Existence is an unformed flow. This flow is mistakenly perceived as the birth and death of many things: thoughts, moods, interests, urges, understandings, bodies, activities, relationships, careers, seasons, planets, galaxies, and so on. These forms don't actually exist; they're like ripples in flowing water.

We can say that every thing is changing, but that isn't accurate, because no form has ever existed that could possibly change. What is, and always has been, is un-form.

In the same way that the movement of nature simply happens, with seasons shifting, rain falling, and flowers growing, the process that we are, our so-called bodily process, mental process, and behavioural process, simply happens.

All that is ever experienced is a mysterious, unformed action. We can't truly describe any qualities, because to identify a quality is to identify form. Even the terms flow, motion, and stream are not describing the presence of any "thing"; they are pointing to un-form.

Existence is not a form of any kind, therefore it's not a sun, a moon, the stars, a person, a body, a mind, a beginning, an ending, a coming, a going, a this world or an other world. It's not a solid, a liquid, or a gas. It is not heat or cold, matter or energy, space or the absence of space. It's not consciousness.

Scientists are forever searching for a particle that makes up the universe, but all they find is process. Now we have quantum physics stating there are no things; there is only process. What *is* can never truly be described because its shape or display never holds still.

We describe our "self" in terms of a body and a mind, but these are more accurately observed as motion. Minds and bodies are constantly altering in gross or subtle ways. Even if we make no effort whatsoever, mental activities continue and bodily processes flow on. Everything ages. That's motion.

We think in terms of various things influencing each other, as though there really are things. We speak of cause and effect, of one thing causing another, or of one thing being affected by another.

But this is like looking at the surface of a river and believing there are various ripples influencing each other. There are no separate ripples. There is only the moving and shifting of one body of water.

In considering this, some will get the impression that we're being pushed around by the flow of nature, but this is not so. Ripples are not pushed around by the movement of water, because ripples *are* the movement.

Try to catch a ripple and all you find is moving water. Try to grab anything in life and all you find is motion that can't be identified as anything in particular.

This movement isn't from a past to a present and a future. The past is the idea that certain forms once existed. The present is the idea that a different set of forms exists now. The future is the idea that still other forms will exist at some point.

But the dance that existence is never has form; it only appears to have form. This deceiving appearance gives the false impression of a past changing to a present and then changing again, to a future. There is no change;

there is always only a mysterious un-form.

This isn't saying that life has no substance: it's saying that what is has no form. Form is an abstraction; it is not real.

We have illusions of form, of self, world, things, free will, determinism, time, space, logic, cause, effect, personal conditioning, purpose, inhibitions, fears, defence mechanisms, insight, understanding, and so on, but none of these actually exist. These descriptions of form are false; they do not apply to what we experience.

Q: *But most of us believe we are some "thing", separate from other things in existence, a thing in a world of things. We believe that we're someone who's capable of manipulating life, someone who's influencing the world around us, someone who is born and will die, someone who has been conditioned by good or bad parenting, someone who's not living up to their potential, someone who needs to do better through his or her efforts, and someone who never feels good enough, but hopes to, in some proposed future.*

DB: Exactly. If those stories are believed, if those false descriptions are believed to be true, there's an incredible amount of emotional anguish that comes with them. If, however, the realization arises that there is no form, then the process of perceiving form, and all the stories about form, are ultimately meaningless.

Thought describes form where no form actually exists, and may be used as a tool when it's helpful, but ignored when it's not. Thought never causes or affects the movement of life; it's merely a tiny portion of that movement.

Thought certainly doesn't describe any truth, so we don't need to obsessively focus on it or lose sleep over it.

If you believe that your descriptions of life are true, then existence will contain a great deal of mental anguish around the story of a poor little you who is struggling in a cold alien world, struggling to understand and control.

You will constantly try to figure it out, to assess it with endless thinking, going to various therapies and therapists, doing various practices, hoping to understand existence, so that somehow you can escape the anguish of your story. But all of this is merely obsessing over the story and the anguish.

If, however, you realize that none of the stories apply, and the tight focus on them falls away, what remains is an amazingly mysterious happening that requires no effort or explanation.

There is simply the unformed, indefinable, pulsing, luminous expression of now.

Nothing born.
Nothing dying.
Nothing incomplete.
Nothing incorrect.
Nothing unfulfilled.

This mysterious happening is not our doing. We, and everything else, are its expression. In this moment it is what it is, and it's unavoidably on its way to a different expression.

There's no possible way of defining it and no possible way of knowing exactly what's coming next.

Q: How would anyone come to see this?

DB: By investigating the present moment.

Sit down, make no effort to breathe, to think, to listen, to feel, or to observe – make no effort to be anything, do anything, or understand anything – and everything happens anyway.

There is only a mysterious happening that has no particular form.

We don't have to spend the rest of our lives sitting still, but it's only when we're doing nothing that it becomes obvious all of existence is moving itself.

And it's only when we stop focusing on the false appearances of form that it becomes obvious existence has no form.

No one has to do it, describe it, or understand it, and it all happens anyway. The breath goes on breathing. The heart goes on beating. The body sensations buzz and swirl. Thoughts go on thinking, moods go on mooding, food digests, hair grows, and the body ages.

At some point, there is a getting up, moving around, eating, sleeping, going to the toilet, making a living, relating to others, and so on. There is this automatic function or expression. It is a process accomplishing itself.

When you wake up in the morning, immediately the process that you are pushes itself forward, with no effort at all. Even the waking up isn't your doing. The particular needs that you are, the particular interests that you are, push themselves forward. All of the interpretations are there, the sense of self, desires, hopes, regrets, urges, and efforts.

But waking has not truly happened. Awareness has not happened. Consciousness has not happened. Knowing has not happened. Body has not happened. Birth has not happened. Sleep has not happened. Parents have not happened. Children have not happened. Conditioning has not happened. Decisions have not happened. Mistakes have not happened. Earth has not happened. Humankind has not happened. These stories are not true.

These are descriptions of form where no form exists.

Q: But I have a husband and children, parents, friends, obligations, a job – I can't just say they don't exist. I can't walk away from all of that. How would I live as a mysterious happening?

DB: There's no problem – you don't have to figure out

how to be the mysterious happening – you're already the mysterious happening, no matter what the situation.

It's not dependent on what you're doing or thinking. The difficulty is not in your particular life situation or in having a story. The difficulty is in believing the stories.

You're able to tell stories based on the apparent forms in a cloud. You could tell stories about them all day long and never think they describe a real world of forms, because it's obviously a cloud and it has no particular shape.

If it becomes obvious that existence has no form, then it doesn't matter if you think in terms of a husband, a wife, children, parents, career, and so on. No matter how much those ideas are there, or how helpful they may be, you will not believe they're truly describing life.

The various storylines automatically present themselves, but they're not true. There's no possible way of knowing what any of this is; we can't even truly say "this is".

Q: *Then how am I supposed to act?*

DB: In whatever way you're expressed. Just be what you are in any particular moment.

The movement that you are is expressing itself right now: the automatic movement of needs, interests, urges, perceptions, thoughts, understandings, abilities, and actions. You're already it. You're not doing it. There is no you who can avoid it or get it wrong. There is only a mysterious river expressing itself.

In any particular moment, there may be numerous urges pulling in many directions, but there will be one particular priority that pushes itself forward, overpowering the others.

Whether it's sitting still, going to the toilet, pursuing a career, chasing a relationship, being confused, or waking from delusion doesn't really matter. All of it is an incomprehensible movement.

We can't say anyone does this dynamic, or directs this dynamic, because all that's ever experienced is this dynamic.

We have absolutely no possible way of knowing what's going on here, but it happens anyway. What arises with this realization is wonder – at the endless mystery of it, the miraculous gifting of it. All of life is a gift.

I'm not saying that with this realization life is always pleasant. It still carries tremendous pains and difficulties.

If the focus does fall away from the stories of form and realizes the indefinable river, there may be a period of fear, sadness, and depression, as belief in the stories fades away.

There may be a sense of losing many valuable things, like self-importance, personal relationship, and control. You might feel there's no point in living. But you will not lose anything valuable. All that's lost is illusion and its related agonies.

As the process continues, the sense of loss is replaced by a sense of wonder and amazement.

Existence is a mysterious gifting. There will be a waiting in wonderment as everything, including the process that you are, simply displays itself. All of life displaying itself with no effort on anyone's part.

External circumstances, and all the internal responses to circumstance, simply happen. It's one mysterious movement.

For the people around you, it will appear as though you lead an ordinary life, more easy-going perhaps, but still exhibiting many qualities that any human being exhibits. For you, however, there is no you, no others, no body, no mind, no world, no doing, no birth, no death, and so on, no sense of fragmentation or lack. There is no obsessive focus on these false ideas.

This is similar to taking your focus away from a movie. If you were in a theatre watching a movie with many other people, all of you would be caught in the thrill of the story, the various characters, the births and deaths, the joys and sorrows, the anxieties and fears, the highs and lows of emotion. You would be absorbed in a story, with all of the wild emotions it produced.

But if your focus falls away from the screen, all of that is gone. Instead, there is a dark room filled with people watching colour dancing on a wall. The movie hasn't ended, but you're no longer focused on that fantasy world. You're not caught in the fantasies and emotions that the others are feeling. There is the impression that the room is the reality, and, compared to the melodrama of the movie, the room is very peaceful.

The movie would continue without your efforts and,

from time to time, it would attract your attention. The fantasy world would arise again. The moving colours once again become a world of people, adventure, crisis, and trauma until that focus falls away.

Even when caught in the movie, and experiencing the wild storm of emotion it generates, you don't take it too seriously, because it's "just" a movie.

It's the same in realizing the unformed, pulsing, luminous, dance of existence. If the focus falls away from thought, and away from the false appearances of form, if it comes to the entire happening of the moment, there is simply an unformed, inexplicable movement.

The thoughts don't end; they continue to happen automatically, a small portion of a larger happening of sights, sounds, touches, tastes, and smells. The dance of light and dark, sound and silence, twinges, pulsations, waves of energy, moods, and so on. All of it, including thought, is a mysterious movement happening on its own.

The thoughts will continue to come and go without effort, and will often be the focus of attention. They will describe their fantasies of form, and may generate wild emotions, but there is the underlying acknowledgment that these stories of form can't possibly be true. They can't be applied to what is.

With complete realization of this, even when the attention gets attracted to the false stories and the wild emotions they generate, none of it is taken too seriously. It's a fantasy.

If the stories of thought are believed to be true, they must generate conflict, because they only function in terms of form, and form doesn't exist. Thought tries to impose form where none exists, to impose understanding where none exists. This imposition is always frustrated, and that's conflict.

If, however, there is only movement, a movement that no one is doing and no one can possibly explain, there can't be any conflict.

It's no more conflicting than lying on a riverbank watching the water flow by. Sometimes the river is wild and raging. Sometimes it's peaceful. In all cases it's a river being a river; it's not a problem.

Life isn't a problem to be understood or solved: it's a river flowing. If for some reason you believe you're separate from it, and that somehow you're doing it, there will be a huge amount of mental anguish.

People generally believe that everything is moved by the laws of nature. We don't believe that planets guide their own orbit or that a bird decides to have a career as a bird. We don't believe that storms decide to be storms or that bears decide to be bears.

We don't believe that a plant, or a rock, is planning how to be a plant or a rock. A plant isn't figuring out how to move as a plant. A rock isn't worrying about whether it's rock-ing correctly. We don't have the impression that it's feeling guilty for being the rock that it is. We believe that everything in existence is moved by the laws of nature. Everything is a movement of the cosmos.

Everything.

Except for us.

For some reason we think we move the cosmos. We think we move our lives. Doesn't that seem strange to you?

Q: It does seem strange, somewhat self-absorbed. Perhaps at this point we could approach the subject of enlightened beings.

DB: Certainly, but I'm wondering if we could continue tomorrow. I'm feeling very tired, and it seems as though we've covered quite a bit today.

Q: *Tomorrow's fine.*

dialogue three

Q: *Good morning.*

DB: Good morning.

Q: *Shall we continue?*

DB: Yes.

Q: *As I said yesterday, I want to get into this matter of enlightened beings.*

DB: In my sense of things, there are no enlightened beings. Once thought realizes its limitations, it doesn't attempt to describe an existence of any kind.
It's just this –

[D gestures to everything around and to his own body.]

There's no interest in defining it.

In my experience, people are always looking for something extraordinary in their spiritual quest: intense concentration, psychic flashes, visions of inner or outer light, energy releases, deep relaxation, special insights, wisdom, compassion, enlightenment, and so on. They believe there's some great freedom to be attained in chasing these things.

For me, these things may be pleasant or interesting if they arise, but they have nothing to do with freedom. Anyone pursuing them is always left yearning for the next special experience, because these things are short-lived.

Special experiences, rushes of energy, visions, insights, and so on, are merely false appearances of form. There's nothing stable in them. There is only an altering that has no particular shape, and we can't possibly grasp it, mentally or physically.

Once it's realized that thoughts can't describe a reality, they are important only as a tool for functioning. Like a hammer. We can use a hammer in many ways, but we wouldn't ask it to describe something called reality, because it can't do that. We can use thought in many ways, but I wouldn't ask it to describe something called reality, because it also can't do that.

Thought still happens, but there's no obsession with its fantasies. There is no desperate urge to explain a reality. There's no impression of knowing anything.

Whether we attempt to describe life or not makes no difference to its movement. It simply moves. We could stand by a river all day long and never attempt to describe it, but the river will flow anyway. The same is true of life, and that flow includes the automatic movement of thought.

Q: *So much for enlightened beings.*

DB: Sorry.

Q: *No, no, it's fine. I'm getting used to this.*

DB: One of the difficulties in relating to this is the desire to reach some goal. Most people think they need to reach some understanding, or get some particular thing, in order to feel complete.

It's my experience that a sense of wholeness is not about gaining anything, or coming to any understanding. When you watch a cloud, you don't need to make that cloud happen. You don't need it to be something in particular. You don't need to understand it as a world of things. It's simply a beautiful and wondrous expression, sometimes dark and stormy, most times big and bouncy. It's the same with all of life.

Everything that has ever occurred has been an indefinable, wondrous expression. It's not, and never was, a bunch of people doing things.

What's fascinating is motion itself. All apparent physical and mental forms simply happen. The process never stops rearranging itself.

Look at the birds and the flowers. Do they have to make effort to get their appearance, their abilities, their circumstances, and their responses to circumstance?

Do birds and flowers have to figure out how to be birds and flowers? They simply are what they are, and it's always changing, automatically. It just happens. It's the same for everything in nature. Why do we think we're expressed in a different way?

Also, look at the lives of some of the great spiritual teachers. Christ was ridiculed, tortured, and died nailed to a cross. The Buddha endured excruciating back pain, famine, attacks from family, attempts on his life, and eventually died of food poisoning, after an extended period of vomiting and diarrhoea.

Why is anyone hoping that their own life is going to be a constantly golden event?

Everything is given, but it's a wide variety of gifts, half of which we don't want. It doesn't really matter what the mind wants. A river flows to its current and not to the wants of a ripple.

Q: *How do I know what's given? What if something's given and I'm not seeing it properly? What if I go in the wrong direction?*

DB: Whatever happens is what's given. We can't go in a wrong direction, because everything we are, and any response we've ever had, is also what's given. Everything you are is an expression of the river.

In my experience, it's incorrect to think that the gift is only the pleasant, the joyful, the clear, the whole, and the kind. All the confusion, sorrow, anger, fragmentation, wars, plagues, famine, and the responses to them, are also the gift.

The many years of yearning, searching, failing, and stumbling in darkness are given, along with periods of clarity, peace, success, and living in the light. That's the full gifting of a rich life.

It's recorded that an old teacher, I think it was Rinzai, could be heard rising in the morning. There were the sounds of a huge belly laugh, shutters being thrown open, and his shouting over the countryside, "What have you got for me today?"

His heart was open to whatever was offered. All of it was a fascinating parade of inexplicable, passing situations, some pleasant, some not, but he had no fear of it, because it was an incomprehensible happening, a mysterious, magical movement, and it included his own being.

We are this mysterious happening and nothing can ever harm it. The false appearances of form come and go; they suffer and die. They can be viewed as adequate or inadequate, successes or failures. But the unformed happening that actually is never comes or goes. It simply is.

Q: *Who's giving the gift?*

DB: A giver, a gift, and a gifting don't actually exist. Life's happening can't be described, but perception and thought refer to it in many ways.

Perception always fantasizes three basic forms: a subject, an object, and some relationship between them. It's the idea of a self, a world, and their relationship. A knower, a known, and a knowing. A giver, a gift, and a gifting. All of it is the same repeating pattern of a subject, an object, and some relationship between them.

This basic illusion of form is found in our sentence structure of subject, object, and verb, but none of these descriptions actually apply to the happening that everyone experiences.

Q: *Could we talk about meditation?*

DB: Certainly.

Q: *What is meditation?*

DB: From this perspective, meditation is the simple expression of the moment. Meditation is the river of now expressing itself, a happening accomplishing itself.

To realize this happening, it's necessary to drop the obsessive focus on the fantasies of doing and thinking. In a period of free time, we set aside any need to be doing and thinking. Nothing needs to be accomplished.

The attention then has permission to rest with the entire happening of the moment. It doesn't need to be focused totally on thought. It can rest with other aspects, like seeing, hearing, touching, tasting, and smelling. Not those words, but the happening they refer to.

Once the narrow focus on doing and thinking is dropped, the broader, mysterious happening of the moment reveals itself.

With a tight focus on thinking and doing, we can never acknowledge life's mysterious movement. Instead, we attach to illusions of form, fragmentation, complexity, control, and conflict.

Only in meditation do we realize an inherent wholeness, simplicity, and ease. There is no other situation that truly moves away from fragmentation, alienation, conflict, struggle, and despair.

When I say meditation, I'm not talking about meditation

techniques, or any particular posture. There are many techniques and postures that people use in an attempt to step out of their fantasies of doing and knowing. But techniques and postures are not meditation.

When we came out of the womb, there were no ideas of a person doing and knowing life. Existence simply expressed itself without interpretation. In meditation there is no need to focus on false stories. There is only motion accomplishing itself, and the passing stories are a portion of that flow.

If this mysterious happening is acknowledged regularly, it becomes increasingly more difficult to define it.

It drops the false assumptions of a self and a world, of knowing and doing. It drops the ideas of an observer and something observed. It drops the ideas of judgment and measurement. There is no success or failure. No awareness.

The focus on these deluded interpretations falls away. Life simply happens without needing to be defined in any way at all. The movement we call perception and thought still happens, but there isn't any obsessive focus on its stories.

It becomes obvious there has never been any "thing"
to describe or define or experience; there is only an
indefinable happening.

Initially, it seems like there is a "me" sitting down to let
this mysterious happening express itself, a "me" sitting to
meditate, but once it's realized there is only indefinable
motion, there is no longer any meditator or meditation.
There is only action. A happening that doesn't need to be
done or understood.

There are so many descriptions: historic, religious,
scientific, new age, philosophic, poetic, spiritual, and
so on. But the obsessive focus on description, and the
belief that it's describing truth, is a huge burden.

Our stories are a pile of dead, rotting leaves compared
to the vital dynamic that life is. Even thinking in terms
of a great cosmos, or cosmic consciousness, is small and
claustrophobic.

We most commonly describe our lives in terms of seeing,
hearing, touching, tasting, smelling, and thinking. Each
of these has an organ related to it: an eye, an ear, a body,
a mouth, a nose, and a brain. And each also has an object
related to it: some "thing" that is seen, heard, touched,

tasted, smelled, or thought.

With these three groups of six forms, we have the complete fantasy of a body, a world, and the relationship between them.

These false forms give the impression of personal doing and knowing, the fantasy of a "me" that is doing and knowing its life. Poetically, you could say each of us carries this six-six-six stamped in our forehead.

The fantasy "me" becomes the centre of a fantasy universe: "I did this; I did that; me first; you can't do that to me; shut up and listen to me; what about me; why me, poor me, only me. Me, me, me. Mine, mine, mine. Gimmee, gimmee, gimmee."

It's the human ego provoking all of its greedy, aggressive, self-absorbed, and self-protective behaviour.

If it's realized that all forms are actually flowing like a river, we're freed from all signs of form, freed from ideas of self, doing, and knowing. These ideas still occur, but there's no belief in them.

Q: *So then, very specifically, where do I find the river?*

Where is the mysterious, unformed, automatic, luminous, pulsing dynamic that you talk about? Where is this movement that's moving itself?

DB: It's the only thing we've ever experienced. It's the only thing we're experiencing now. It's this moment.

Sit down and do nothing; you don't even have to focus on thinking and observing. The moment doesn't disappear or fall apart when you make no effort to do it or describe it or observe it. It simply presents itself, without effort on anyone's part.

Everything is altering. In our daily lives, this isn't immediately obvious, because much of the altering is very slow. When our eyes are open, we're focused mainly on that slow movement and it appears to be unchanging.

For example, this house we're sitting in: it doesn't immediately strike you that it has no form. But if you consider that this house, over a long period of time, will eventually dry up, turn to dust, and blow away – that it's not remaining new for hundreds of years and then growing old overnight – you realize it's changing now. It doesn't have any particular form right now.

If we sit and close our eyes, or lower our gaze away from visual forms, the changing quality of existence is obvious. Movement makes itself known in the shifting thoughts, emotions, sounds, tastes, smells, waves of energy, pulsations, vibrations, and so on, that make up the now.

Even the attention is dancing around. Everything is doing this on its own. You can't truly describe it as anything in particular.

Everything in this ordinary moment is the mysterious, unformed, indescribable river.

Since it has no particular form, we could say it's pulsing, radiant, and luminous. These words give a sense of motion. Tactile and visual motion.

If I speak of a mysterious, unformed, automatic, radiant, luminous, pulsing expression, it's difficult to make any particular form out of it, or any particular thing to cling to. Instead, it gives a sense of action, motion, or dance. I could just call it un-form, but this is an invitation to explore, and it seems more inviting to step into radiant luminescence than it is to step into un-form.

Ultimately, my descriptions are false too, but they invite you to step out of description, in order to experience a sense of freedom and well-being that is impossible to create or to understand. There is an incredible sense of freedom and well-being in all of this. It's similar to waking up after a night of deep sleep.

In deep sleep we give up everything. There is no knowing or doing, no wanting, and no possessing. There are no ideas of awareness or observing.

The experience of that, upon waking in the morning, is a feeling of peace and well-being. That sense of peace and well-being is inherent in the process we are. We don't need to create it.

My words invite you to step out of the focus on doing and thinking, to experience a freedom and joy that can't be found in any other way. This is the absence of a tight, constricted focus on false views. It's also the absence of the fears and desperate searching that focus produces.

It may be realized that everything rolls along quite fine without attempting to focus on doing and thinking. There is a mysterious, indescribable, rolling along. Ideas automatically arise when needed, and our actions do too.

Our appearance, direction, and actions simply happen. This realization is freedom. From that point on, there is no meditator, no meditation, no doing, no knowing, and no realization. There is only a mysterious happening that can't be understood in any way. It becomes obvious there has never been anything else.

This is a complete opening to the unformed, the undirected, the uncontrolled, the unexpected, and the unpredictable. This openness is often called love. In this, you are not a body; you are not a mind; there is only love.

This love is not some cold, intellectual understanding; it's an openness of heart. This love is not an aching, desire-filled attachment to a person, a possession, an idea, a cause, a career, a practice, or an understanding.

This love is not some romantic myth of everyone embracing and singing the same song. Instead, it's a truly sensitive vulnerability to what is.

Ideas only go so far. At some point, the heart may open to the totally indefinable, unpredictable, and often unwanted movement that life is. Love is that openness of heart.

You could say that most of us attempt to refuse the gift of existence, because there is a fear of the unexpected and the possibly painful.

There is a great amount of tension in this refusal, and all it ever produces is a feeling of general upset. The attempt to refuse the river of life is futile. There is nothing separate from it that could ever refuse it.

Q: *People in spiritual circles often use the word liberation. In your experience, what gets liberated?*

DB: Nothing, because nothing has ever been in bondage. The entire story of a journey from ignorance to enlightenment is a fantasy. It doesn't matter what we think; none of the stories apply.

Q: *I know that a number of people have asked you to write down your own life story, but you won't do it. Why?*

DB: Because it puts the focus back on delusions of thought. I'm inviting you to a freedom from that delusion. Why would I turn anyone back to the fantasies that create their mental anguish and conflict?

Q: *But if you gave your life story, people would see that*

your journey hasn't been easy, in the same way it hasn't been easy for them.

DB: The bookshops are already filled with stories of difficult lives. I'm pointing to something else.

Q: *But many would like to hear your story.*

DB: Yes, but I'm pointing to a peace and well-being that reveals itself only when the focus on stories is dropped.

In that, the illusions of your personal journey, conflict, and mental anguish may fade away. But you'll never find out unless you step away from the stories.

Q: *Perhaps we could address another issue. You seem to have something against spiritual practices and I'd like to look at that.*

DB: I have nothing against them. But in my experience, a real sense of freedom and joy has nothing to do with practicing anything, or developing anything.

Somehow, there's a general impression that this is about practicing awareness or concentration, trying to become more aware, more skilled at paying attention, clinging to a particular focus, clinging to the present, clinging to the breath, clinging to physical sensations, clinging to concentration. Or there's the impression it's about developing another insight or endless kindness.

The freedom I'm pointing to is not about developing awareness, concentration, insight, or anything else. It's not about practicing or developing anything. It's not about self-improvement.

Don't you complain about things changing? The weather, your relationship, your health, your job, your friends, your thoughts, and so on?

Q: *Yes, everyone does.*

DB: Exactly. To some extent, most people already see the river. They're complaining because it's moving beyond control. They're already seeing the mysterious, unformed motion that life is.

They've never experienced anything else. But most people refuse to acknowledge it to that degree. They prefer to cling to ideas of personal doing and control.

Meditation simply lets the focus fall away from appearances of form and acknowledges constant motion. If you sit and do absolutely nothing for a period of time each day, motion becomes obvious. Inside, outside, everywhere.

That indefinable action is all that is.

Q: *But if I don't make an effort to do anything, I could end up catatonic, sitting around all the time, not responding to anything at all.*

DB: Try it. Try not responding to anything at all. Try giving up everything that makes sense to you, everything you value, everything you care for.

You may be able to restrain your urges temporarily, but they will eventually push through because, each time life offers a particular set of circumstances, it also offers your response to those circumstances, the response that makes most sense to you or feels right to you. It's forever altering in some way but, in each instance, there is one response that ultimately pushes itself forward.

Traumatic situations contain a storm of contradictory feelings and urges, and the opinions of others may be added to the mix but, out of that storm, one response will ultimately push through.

If we attempt to repress that response, it produces conflict. If we attempt that kind of control, we'll eventually experience confusion, stomach aches, headaches, depression, and exhaustion – and this emotional turmoil will eventually reveal our true feelings.

This doesn't mean that we express every passing whim or emotion, but certain ones are more persistent than others and they become the expression of our lives. A moment of anger may not need to be expressed, but an ongoing feeling of anger, or unhappiness, will eventually make itself known. It's the same with all emotion.

In each moment, your circumstances are given and your response to circumstance is also given. This will be followed by other circumstances and responses. It's one seamless movement. It's a fascinating parade of appearances and there's no way of knowing exactly what's coming next.

This is a multi-dimensional entertainment system, with the automatic appearance of sights, sounds, touches,

tastes, smells, thoughts, urges, activities, adventures,
traumas, confusion, clarity, joy, and sorrow.

All of that. And more.

Just do whatever makes the most sense to you in any
particular moment. Everything you are comes together
physically, mentally, emotionally, psychologically,
and spiritually, a million nuances in alignment with
a particular set of circumstances, because it's one
movement.

You're expressed in whatever way you're expressed. All of
existence is this mysterious river of expression. Maybe
you'll sit and do nothing, or maybe you'll go for a five
mile run, or maybe you'll try to end world hunger. Who
knows? The river flows in whatever way it flows. It's
filled with surprises.

You don't have to make yourself obey the river of life:
there's nothing but the river. There has never been
anything else. The ego is a movement in that river.
Sit down, do nothing, and old man river, or old crone
river, just keeps rolling along.

If this action reveals itself clearly then all personal doing and knowing comes to an absolute end. We're cast upon the waters of un-form. In losing our life this way, losing the false notions of being, owning, doing, and knowing, we find everything simply offered in a miraculous movement.

If it's acknowledged fully, that there is only a great, mysterious river, there will be no need of psychological protection or justification. There's no need to protect your image, or justify your existence, if there is only a mysterious motion expressing itself.

The basic physical survival mechanisms still function, but there is no need of ego protection. Pride, rationalization, justification, clinging, greed, aggression, arrogance, self-pity, and so on, fade away.

We normally compare our "self" to others, thinking that we're either inadequate or superior. Usually, it's a sense of inadequacy.

We imagine countless situations that are better than ours and attempt to wilfully impose them on the flow of life. But they will only happen if that's what the river is offering, and there's no way of predicting exactly what the process will offer.

Q: *You're so certain of this. It makes sense to me, but I don't have that certainty.*

DB: As far as I can tell, you can't find this certainty in words. It's found only in acknowledging motion. This means stepping out of thoughts and wilful actions to simply rest as the unprovoked happening of the moment. There is nothing to get, nothing to do, and nothing to understand.

It's not about practicing something for an hour in order to be able to see motion for a few minutes. There's never anything but motion. Sit down and let it reveal itself.

Maybe it's restless and irritated. Maybe it's calm. Maybe it's angry. Maybe it's peaceful. Maybe it's sad. Maybe it's happy. Maybe thoughts are coming by the millions. Maybe there are no thoughts. Whatever it is is changing and there's no way to stop it. It's happening on its own.

Leave it alone and it reveals its own natural order. In no longer wrestling with it, no longer wanting it to be different, no longer trying to do it or direct it, no longer trying to understand it, there is a great sense of peace and the growing faith that you don't ever have to wrestle with it. Because it simply moves to its own rhythm and current. It always has.

It's a miraculous expression, and we're simply expressed.

At first, we test this in a safe place, a quiet room, alone, or with those we can trust, but soon it's apparent in all activities. Everything is a mysterious process carrying itself along.

If you want to learn about life then watch it flow, just as you would sit on a riverbank watching the water flow by. The water of now is the shift and dance of sights, sounds, touches, tastes, smells, thoughts, moods, and so on.

You may notice that the watcher is flowing, as body sensations rise and pass, the breath comes and goes, and the heart beats. There is vibration, pulsation, waves of energy, heat, coolness, heaviness, lightness, a little pain here, a little shift there.

You may further notice that the observing is flowing, as attention dances around, one moment with the breath, the next, sound, the next, sight, the next, touch, and so on. Sometimes clear and sometimes dull.

Soon it's obvious there is only motion, and it no longer makes sense to describe the ripples of the moment or get caught up in them.

Ultimately, this river can't be understood. It's totally baffling. In absolute puzzlement, it's free of all ideas of awareness, pure awareness, observing, self, world, doing, knowing, and being.

There's no attempt to do anything, know anything, or be anything, and, surprisingly, life happens anyway.

What's even more surprising is that nothing important is lost. Instead, things like fear, greed, condemnation, anger, argument, doubt, alienation, and loneliness melt away.

Old habits in these areas may still arise, but it becomes increasingly more difficult to sustain them. It's different for each person.

Q: *So others are experiencing this freedom. The people you teach?*
DB: Yes. But it's not a matter of teaching anyone how to be free. It depends on whether or not someone inherently resonates with this sense of life.

For those who do, the self is immediately removed from the centre of existence, without any effort to do so. It's simply the realization that this old perspective is false.

I can't create anyone's potential for relating to this. All I can do is point to a few observable facts.

For some, those facts are merely a curiosity; they're not incredibly significant. For others, when they see what I'm pointing to, the sense of life shifts radically. From then on, their personal stories of confusion and angst start melting away, automatically.

Q: *Is this the freedom described in the teachings of Buddhism, Taoism, Advaita, and some others?*

DB: It certainly seems so, according to various accounts, but there are always those who would argue against that.

For me, this question isn't important. What's important is your experience of life right now.

I'm asking if everything that you know of is constantly changing.

I'm asking you if that's true. It's a very simple question.

I'm also asking you if the changing is occurring on its own.

If you sit down and make no effort to do anything or be anything, does life's movement still occur, including the process that you are?

If the answer to these questions is yes, then it follows that existence, in all of your experience, is indefinable motion accomplishing itself.

Is that your experience?

If it is, you're immediately outside of everything that anyone has ever said. Every statement ever made about existence is ultimately unimportant. Including mine. Descriptions don't apply.

What remains is wonder and amazement. It's the same sense of wonder you might experience under a huge, star-filled, night sky. As you look up, the beauty and immensity of that happening is indescribable; thought is completely baffled, leaving only a sense of awe.

It's possible to have that sense of wonder when you're washing the dishes, or looking in the bathroom mirror, or having a thought, because even the most ordinary moment is that same incomprehensible happening.

Most of us focus on fantasies and believe they're true. The great and wondrous river of existence is ignored in a desperate clinging to conflict-ridden, ego-bound stories of form.

If you ever acknowledge the river fully – even once – those delusions can't maintain themselves.

in a different fashion

All is un-form,
absence of message,
absolute puzzlement.

And this gives rise to apparent beginnings.

In beginnings is logos,
the image and description of form.
And logos is with mystery
and logos is mystery.
And logos masks the waters of un-form.

Fantasies of form
gauge and measure un-form,
and they fall.

For in judging and measuring un-form,
they are measured and judged.

Compared and found lacking.
Separated and made lonely.

They fall, in snaking tales,
"my" birth, "my" death, "my" struggle, "my" pain,
"my" rights. Hisst-story, the worship of form,
idol.

Images of birth and death.
Of hardship and woe.
Of desertion and betrayal.
Of plagues, and wars, and famine.
Of wandering in barren lands.
Of search, and hope, and despair.

Vanity, vanity, all is vanity.

Matter and flesh is flowing.
Go down to that river to bathe.
Cast your self on the waters of un-form,
and be cleansed.

In a quiet place, open, not as matter or flesh,
but as motion.

Be still and realize. Your bodies are streaming.

The cosmos' great city is river-ing.

All is streaming.

Form washes clean.

All is un-form.

And dwells in the house of wonder.

L's ps

[*apologies James Joyce*]

All my leaves have drifted from me.
But one clings still. Love.
I'll bear it to remind me,
 so soft these mornings of ours.
Carry me along Daddy, through hushed grass,
like you did through the toy fair.
Take, but softly, memory me,
'til "thou" ends all "the",
 and the keys are given.
Away loneliness! At last love.
Along the
 riverrun.

[*Finnegans Wake*, last page]

acknowledgments
and appreciation

My thanks to Sandra Stuart, Link Phillips, Karen
Clements, Brenda Reimer-Dorratt, Sally Perchaluk,
Juliette Sabot, Dale Purvis, Bob Hamilton, Dale Ingram,
Jon Mousley, Frances Wright, Keith Millan, Dianne
Wilt, Nick Herzmark, Śakti Rose, and Valerie Metcalfe,
for their reflections on the early rough expression of this
work.

I want to voice my special gratitude to Sandra Stuart and
Link Phillips, having been my partners through the birth
of two books and the remodelling of another. It has been
my pleasure to have their company, their friendship, and
the support of their respective talents.

It was in conversations with Sandra that I first expressed
my views openly. Subsequently, she offered both the
encouragement and opportunity to share them with
others.

Support for this expression has appeared in many
guises. To mention a few more:

My mother, Gwen, my father, Ed, and my brother, Brent.

J. Krishnamurti, Ruth Denison, Ajahn Sumedho, and Robert Adams.

Alan Watts, Ramesh Balsekar, and U.G.

Mary Wall, Toan Tran, Anna Millan, Jill Osler, Sheilagh Konyk, Ruth Wood, Norma Nickson, Wendy Rondeau, Gordon Hargreaves, Joan Tollifson, and Julian Noyce.

NON-DUALITY PRESS

If you enjoyed this book, you might be interested in these related titles published by Non-Duality Press.

CONSCIOUS.TV

CONSCIOUS.TV is a TV channel broadcasting on the Internet at www.conscious.tv. Certain programmes are also broadcast on Satellite TV stations based in the UK. The channel aims to stimulate debate, question, enquire, inform, enlighten, encourage and inspire people in the areas of Consciousness, Healing and Psychology.

There are already over 100 interviews to watch including several with communicators on Non-Duality including Gangaji, Jeff Foster, Catherine Noyce, Richard Lang, Roger Linden, Tony Parsons, Halina Pytlasinska, Genpo Roshi, Richard Sylvester, Rupert Spira, Florian Schlosser, Francis Lucille, and Pamela Wilson. Some of these interviewees also have books available from Non-Duality Press.

Do check out the channel as we are interested in your feedback and any ideas you may have for future programmes. Email us at info@conscious.tv with your ideas or if you would like to be on our email newsletter list.

WWW.CONSCIOUS.TV

CONSCIOUS.TV and *NON-DUALITY PRESS*
present two unique DVD releases

CONVERSATIONS ON NON-DUALITY – VOLUME 1

Tony Parsons – *The Open Secret* • Rupert Spira –
The Transparency of Things – Parts 1 & 2 • Richard Lang –
Seeing Who You Really Are

CONVERSATIONS ON NON-DUALITY – VOLUME 2

Jeff Foster – *Life Without a Centre* • Richard Sylvester –
I Hope You Die Soon • Roger Linden – *The Elusive Obvious*

Available to order from: www.non-dualitypress.com

Lightning Source UK Ltd.
Milton Keynes UK
UKOW050611090912

198673UK00001B/35/P